Alphabets and Designs for Wood Signs

Alphabets and Designs for Wood Signs

Patrick and Sherri Spielman

Home Craftsman Series

STERLING PUBLISHING CO., INC.   New York

Metric Conversion Chart

⅛ inch = 3.18 millimetres	⅝ inch = 15.88 millimetres	1½ inch = 38.10 millimetres
¼ inch = 6.35 millimetres	¾ inch = 19.05 millimetres	2 inches = 50.80 millimetres
⅜ inch = 9.53 millimetres	⅞ inch = 22.23 millimetres	1 foot = 30.48 centimetres
½ inch = 12.70 millimetres	1 inch = 25.40 millimetres	1 yard = 0.9144 metre
	10 millimetres = 1 centimetre	

Library of Congress Cataloging in Publication Data

Spielman, Patrick E.
    Alphabets and designs for wood signs.

    (Home craftsman series)
    Includes index.
    1. Woodwork.   2. Signs and sign-boards.   3. Alphabets.
4. Decoration and ornament.   I. Spielman, Sherri.
II. Title.   III. Series.
TT200.S58   1983   674'.88   83-507
ISBN 0-8069-5482-5
ISBN 0-8069-7702-7 (pbk.)

Fifth Printing, 1986

© 1983 by Patrick and Sherri Spielman
Published by Sterling Publishing Co., Inc.
Two Park Avenue, New York, N.Y. 10016
Distributed in Canada by Oak Tree Press Ltd.
℅ Canadian Manda Group, P.O. Box 920, Station U
Toronto, Ontario, Canada M8Z 5P9
Distributed in the United Kingdom by Blandford Press
Link House, West Street, Poole, Dorset BH15 1LL, England
Distributed in Australia by Capricorn Ltd.
P.O. Box 665, Lane Cove, NSW 2066

Table of Contents

Acknowledgments

The authors dedicate this book to "Mrs. Pat," mother, wife, and business partner; a woman of many great talents. We do thank her for the artistic contributions to this book, but more importantly we acknowledge with enduring respect and appreciation the overall support, encouragement, and love we have enjoyed throughout all of our years together.

We do want to acknowledge the suggestions and contributions afforded to us by many friends and colleagues in the wood sign business. Their many letters and phone calls were guiding factors for us, and they all were supportive of this effort. First, we want to give special thanks to Tod Swormsstedt, editor of *Signs of the Times* magazine. He supplied many excellent photos from his publication's sign competitions and diligently helped us to meet some pressing deadlines. A very special thanks to Mike Jackson from Moore, Oklahoma. Mike's work is highly visible throughout the pages of this book and we consider it an honor to have his work illustrated here because he is certainly one of the real pros and the most energetic in the business.

Similarly, we thank these professionals for some excellent illustrations: Dick Malacek, Bill Schnute, Don Davis, Wayne Detjen, Carl Rauwerdink, and Don Zinngrabe, along with many other individuals whose signs are pictured in this book.

Thanks to Dominick Parisi of Spanjer Brothers, Inc., to John Middlebrooks of Anchor Continental, Inc., and to James M. Fassett II of Integrated Laser Systems, Inc. for allowing us to use some of the illustrations from their companies' literature.

Finally, we thank our own customers, for keeping us active with wood signs.

Introduction

The public's appreciation and demand for authentic artistically handcrafted wood signs have increased very rapidly in recent years. In fact, many large municipalities, subdivisions, conservatories, parks, and small resort villages have established or are establishing ordinances prohibiting metal, neon, and lighted plastic signs. See Illustrations 1 and 2. Personalized wood signs for the home, business, farm, and estate are being seen more and more (Illus. 3). This perpetuates interest and increases the demand for the talents of the wood sign artist. Consequently, the sign craftsman needs new ideas and some fresh approaches to avoid duplication and monotony in his products and services.

Since the 1981 publication of our book *Making Wood Signs* (Sterling Publishing Co.), we have had hundreds of calls and letters requesting more alphabet patterns, new design ideas, and additional information pertaining to the business aspects of wood sign work.

This book, though not all-inclusive, is an attempt to satisfy those requests. It is prepared essentially for those individuals who have mastered the basics of *Making Wood Signs* and for those who are so caught up in this fascinating craft that they can "taste" the commercial potential it has to offer.

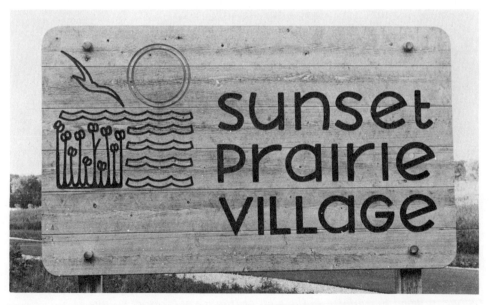

Illus. 1. Exclusive developments and entire villages are turning to wood signs.

It has been especially gratifying to learn of the fast rate of success many craftsmen have experienced since picking up their copy of *Making Wood Signs*.

Included in this volume are lots of different alphabets. These are adapted from various sources, primarily typeface and dry-transfer-lettering catalogs. They have been selected and modified for suitability to wood sign crafting. Some are more appropriate for routing and carving while others are better suited to sand-blasting. There are plenty of choices to add variety and spice to your specialized area. Alphabets, in themselves, cannot be copyrighted, but descriptive names can be. So, for obvious and practical reasons the alphabets in this book are not identified by specific names.

Along with the new alphabet patterns are some symbols, designs, decorations, and border ideas. These designs and patterns may also be useful to you in other areas of handicrafts such as leatherworking, woodcrafts, glass etching, and so on.

Included, too, are numerous photos of superb wood signs generously provided by many different wood sign professionals. Among these photos are some of the design winners from national competitions. The photos are unselfishly provided as a source of inspiration and ideas to help you plan and execute your own wood signs. Those signs not otherwise identified were fabricated by the author.

All craftsmen need to view and study the works of others to learn new tech-niques and approaches. This helps to develop and enrich your own skills and capabilities. We do not advocate copying another's sign in detail. However, modi-

Illus. 2. This sign, usually seen in an internally lighted plastic version, was redone in wood to conform to the sign ordinance of a resort village.

Illus. 3. Residential signs in wood are gaining in popularity.

fication, both by changing the overall configuration and combining desirable elements taken from a number of different signs, is fairly common practice. You will note, by looking at the photos throughout this book, a trend towards combining two or more wood sign techniques (router work, hand carving, cutout work, sandblasting, painted art, airbrush work, etc.) into one sign. The ever higher levels of design and technique offer many challenges and opportunities for the creative and enterprising craftsman involved in making wood signs.

Overview and Update

Design Enlargement and Modification

Every good sign begins with a good design (Illus. 4 and 5). The more you become involved with sign work, the more you will be called upon to suggest and produce designs for your clients. The need to design becomes increasingly important, not only to satisfy the varied needs of your customers, but also to satisfy yourself. It is immensely rewarding to work out a design and produce a sign after conferring with the client to determine what is actually wanted in terms of size, finances, and other limitations.

The ideal jobs are those in which the financial restrictions take a back seat to artistic fruition. The sad fact of the matter is that most prospects expect more than they are at first willing to pay for. Whenever the opportunity does come along to do a super job—namely, one without rigid price restraints—it is wise to

Illus. 4. This large highway-type sign by Mike Jackson is an excellent example of the overall beauty that can be achieved in designing wood signs.

Illus. 5. Another contemporary wood sign by Mike Jackson. The unusual design features vertical planking with integral post work.

do the very best, giving more than is expected not only in the designing, but also in the making. Having such signs out in the public's view will be your best advertising. They will enhance your reputation. Your new prospects will give you a freer rein and you will command their respect when discussing and designing signs.

Essentially, design in sign work involves delivering the appropriate graphic message by attracting the viewer's attention in a positive manner. The overall appearance should do everything possible to enhance the function of the sign. A very ornate and overly decorative sign, for example, may defeat the primary functions of clarity and easy readability.

A fundamental premise is to be basic and bold. Remember that a commercial highway sign must "deliver" its message very quickly because the viewer is travelling past at high speed. Indoor signs, such as those in malls and shopping centers, can be handled differently since the viewer, who is on foot, has more time to absorb additional artistic touches and wordier messages.

Study the very large billboards along the public highways. You will note that the messages are basic, usually consisting of only the few necessary words despite the sign's extremely large size.

The major problem is getting the right idea across to clients interested in the large-size signs. They think the sign, because it is large in size, should carry more than the basic message. Because they are investing in a big sign there is room for everything: business hours, address, phone numbers, and the complete menu, too.

You should make a careful analysis of your design to be sure that the sign actually does what it is intended to do. For example, is the lettering legible or would another lettering style be easier to read? Script and Old English letters

Illus. 6 (top left). An example of an appropriate typeface, carrying out the western theme. Note how the letters are sized to make optimum use of the space.

Illus. 7 (above). This large sign by Paul Reinhard is a good application of a modified Old English. This lettering style creates a feeling of long establishment and tradition.

Illus. 8 (left). This good-looking sign by Mike Jackson is an example of dramatic results achieved through simplicity.

EL TORITO
MEXICAN FOOD

Illus. 9. This decorative lettering is certainly appropriate for a Mexican restaurant. Note that these two different type styles are effectively used, providing emphasis and contrast. Note, also, that even though the letters and lines are close together, the message is still easy to read.

are more difficult to read than most other alphabets. Avoid using complex, decorative typefaces on signs that require maximum legibility. On the other hand, the extremes of "balloon fat" or heavy bold letters do not read as easily as letters of medium line-thickness or stroke-width. When selecting an alphabet with a decorative face, be very cautious—the letter design should convey the appropriate feeling and meaning. See Illustrations 6–9 for some examples.

Other questions in analyzing sign designs include: Is too much design crammed into the space? Would more background space improve the overall appearance? (See Illus. 8.) Are words and phrases laid out so they can be read with a sensible meaning? (Be careful when separating words or phrases into different lines. The words in each line must read clearly and be meaningful together.) Does the sign have sufficient contrast to be legible?

The proper use of color is an effective way to achieve contrast. Backgrounds should be of a contrasting color to that of the letters and designs. Remember that light-colored letters against a dark background appear larger than the same-size letters painted dark against a light background. Contrast or emphasis can also be achieved by using different-size letters to draw the eye to the key word or phrase of the message. Avoid using too many different type styles on the same sign, however. Trying to create some variety and interest may be a good idea, but combinations of several letter styles are more likely to create an element of confusion than a feeling of consistency and unity.

Observation, with an analytical eye, of all forms or areas of the graphic arts will be of immense value to the designer of wood signs. Look at newspaper and magazine ads, and run through the yellow pages. You will quickly notice the sharp, eye-catching designs incorporated into the logos and identifying artwork of the large companies and progressive small businesses. You may notice also that many current graphic artists and advertising illustrators use similar techniques. For example, they tend to space letters very closely together, much

Illus. 10. The problem, shown at the top, is that the desired letter height does not fit the horizontal space. The solution is either (left) to reduce the size or (right) to condense the letter width to fit the space.

more closely now than was the accepted practice a few years back. Letters often touch each other, as do words and lines of words—some even overlapping. This technique gives the designer the opportunity to use large letters in otherwise tight areas.

Of course, there is more to designing wood signs than simply enlarging letters from alphabet patterns. This is not to say that nice signs cannot be made simply by the use of "as is" enlarged letters along with a suitable design set to a side or corner of the sign. Often you and your client will agree during the initial stages of your conference that the letters should be a certain specific height for optimum visibility. However, as you work out the design you find that the letters do

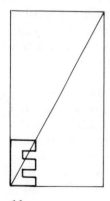

Illus. 11. The diagonal line method quickly determines height-to-width ratio for enlarging letters.

not fit horizontally in the space available. The option then is to either reduce the size of the letters or condense them. See Illustration 10.

One quick way of determining the proportional horizontal space that will be required for letters enlarged to a specific height is to use the diagonal line method. For example, if you wanted to enlarge a letter (as printed in this book) to a height of six inches, draw a horizonal line six inches above and parallel to the base line. Then draw a diagonal line through the letter (or through an imaginary rectangular space surrounding the letter) until it intersects the top horizontal line. Complete the rectangle, as shown in Illustration 11.

Enlarging the letter and design patterns from this book can be handled by the same graph-square or grid system commonly used by woodworkers to enlarge their project patterns. Inclined letters can be created by enlarging the original on a slanted grid, and the grid system can also be used to make condensed or expanded letters from any original pattern. See Illustrations 12 and 13.

The enlarging methods using opaque or overhead projectors, as described in the book *Making Wood Signs*, are valuable timesaving techniques worth checking into. However, these systems do have some limitations where extreme accuracy and freedom from distortion are absolutely necessary.

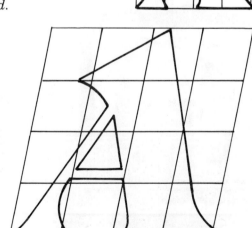

Illus. 12. Enlarging by the grid or graph-square method. The original is at the right. Below left is a straight enlargement and below right is an enlargement with a design modification using a slanted grid.

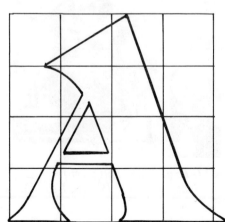

15

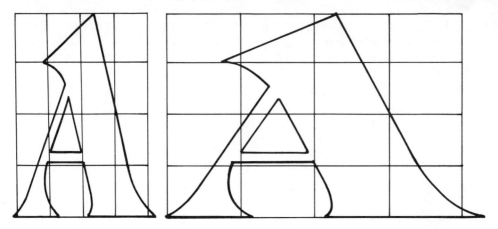

Illus. 13. The graph-square method can be modified by using rectangular grids to (left) enlarge and condense or (right) enlarge and expand the original example in Illustration 12.

Do not fabricate a sign if it is not a good design. Your reputation and your future hang delicately by the thread of good design. Regardless of how well you craft a sign with good, expert woodworking skills, its overall value and the appraisal of your work are drastically overshadowed by design quality. If you cannot create a good design it is best to inform your client that you have drawn a blank on the project and you need to engage the services of a professional artist with such-and-such fees to be charged to the invoice. Or, give the client the option of securing his own designer to work with you, so you can handle the technical and structural aspects of the sign. In this way you are telling your

Illus. 14. Examples of clip art from Dynamic Graphics, Inc., Peoria, Illinois.

client that you are conscientious and openly concerned about wanting him to have the very best sign possible.

In addition to the option of engaging a professional artist yourself, you might want to look into mail order professional design and pattern services. Clip art is one such service that print shops, advertising agencies, artists, and designers use themselves. Clip art (examples shown in Illus. 14) is available both in book form and by monthly subscriptions. These services offer a vast source of art for such design elements as borders, letterheads, line art, and so on. All art is created by top contemporary illustrators, designers, and lettering stylists.

Full-size patterns custom-developed for your signs can also be ordered by mail. Precise letter designs, symbols, and borders for any sign from one inch to 100 feet in height can be obtained in full size from companies specializing in this service. One such company, called "The Pattern Man," a division of Integrated Laser Systems, Inc., based in San Marcos, California, employs a computer graphics system in its work. All you do is send in the general specifications, including the overall size, the copy, the letter style, art for symbols or logos, and the general layout with preferred letter heights. This information is fed into a computer and you get a full-size print (pattern) by return mail. It will have the letters expanded or condensed (as necessary), aligned, and spaced perfectly while maintaining the original design concept.

This is a much more precise system of enlargement than either grid-aided freehand enlargement or the projector blow-up method. The projector blow-up method is very susceptible to distortion. When enlarging a company's logo, it is most essential that the enlargement be perfectly accurate, free from distortion, and with the proportions and visual impact unchanged.

If your sign requires individual cutout letters and designs, from plywood or other sheet materials, you can also order a "cutting nest" pattern. This has all of the characters needed to make the sign arranged in an efficient layout for optimum, conservative use of the sheet material. See Illustration 15. You can also order a complete font of letters in any desired style or size.

Illus. 15. A cutting nest pattern.

Illus. 16. Some examples of cutout letters.

Cutout Letters and Designs

Crafting individual letters (Illus. 16) or designs and attaching them to a flat panel is perhaps the easiest way to create a dimension of depth in wood signs. A lot can be done with a minimum of tools and equipment. The attractive, contemporary sign shown in Illustration 17 was made using only an electric sabre saw (or coping saw). The letters and ornaments were cut from exterior plywood.

Using a router, you can round over or cove-cut the edges of letters that have been cut from solid wood. This adds more interest and professionalism. The faces of cutout letters can also be decorated by router carving or sandblasting.

The idea of decorating or working the faces of letters can be carried even further. Some very distinctive letters can be made by hand carving and sculpturing the faces. One company still specializing today in handcrafted, ornamental, carved wood letters is Spanjer Brothers, Inc. of Chicago. This company has been in existence, hand carving letters and wood decor, since 1896. That they have enjoyed continuous business all these years attests to the public's long-standing acceptance and demand for handcrafted woodwork in signage. With the current trend towards "real" wood, coupled with the present popularity of historical restorations, their business is going strong. Spanjer Brothers supplies solid wood sculptured letters in all sizes (Illus. 18 and 19) to other sign companies that do not have the capability to craft their own.

Illustration 20 shows close-up details of a sign fabricated by Mike Jackson. This sign incorporates applied carving and letter work in an unusual design and dramatically illustrates the creative imagination of the sign artist. Now, is there a client that wouldn't be tickled pink to be able to purchase a sign like that?

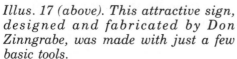

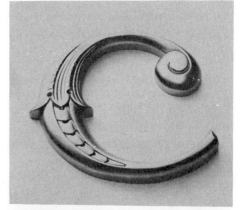

Illus. 17 (above). This attractive sign, designed and fabricated by Don Zinngrabe, was made with just a few basic tools.

Illus. 18 (top right). Wood letters of any size and look are handmade by Spanjer Brothers, Inc.

Illus. 19 (middle right). An example of the fine work done at Spanjer Brothers, Inc.

Illus. 20 (bottom right). Close-up showing Mike Jackson's work. Cutout letters and carving were applied to a carved, textured background.

Illus. 21. Example of a freehand routed sign. A round-bottom bit was used to cut each letter with one stroke (or pass) of the router, producing the finished depth and width of the letter face. The design was shallow-outlined with a "V" bit.

Routing

The basics of sign routing are covered in our previous book *Making Wood Signs*. Please refer to it if you need to review the aspects of bit selection, freehand router manipulation (Illus. 21), guided router work (Illus. 22 and 23), and so on.

One thing that clearly distinguishes the work of an amateur from that of a pro in commercial sign work is the depth of cut. Most beginners do not rout deep. Deeply routed letters add greatly to the drama and overall visual impact because of the interplay of light and shadow. Generally, the larger the sign, the larger the letters, and the deeper they should be cut. Deep routing requires

Illus. 22. This yet-to-be-painted sign was produced by a combination of routing techniques. The straight vertical line cuts of the letters were made by guiding the router with a T-square. The horizontal straight lines (letter tops and bottoms) were cut following a straightedge clamped to the work. The same was done for the straight cuts of the design. The circle was outlined using a router compass attachment. The curved letters were cut freehand with a narrow bit and widened with successive passes, working outward to the layout lines.

Illus. 23. A closeup look at the router work from Illustration 22. Note the nice depth of cut and the resultant accent of light and shadow.

sharp bits and "power"—meaning not only the router's horsepower, but the physical power and strength of the operator as well. The router must be guided along its intended path surely and confidently. One slip or moment of relaxation could ruin the workmanship and thus require a patch, inlay, or replaced board.

Obviously, deep-cut letters and art can often be made with two or more passes at shallower depths. This technique is certainly the one to use whenever conveniently possible. There are times, however, when it can't be done with multiple passes, especially when large areas must be totally cut away, thus removing the area that normally supports the router base. This problem occurs when cutting away large areas of background in relief router work or when engraving very large letters that have wide, fat faces such as shown in Illustration 24.

Illus. 24. Routing wide and deep. Caution must be exercised to prevent the router from dropping into the area already cut away.

Illus. 25. Taking a pass at less than the full depth can be accomplished by tipping the router, as shown. Note that the operator is keeping the router a safe distance from the layout line.

Illus. 26. Another view of the same operation. These deep outlining cuts could be made in several shallow cutting passes with the router base always resting flat. However, when making frequent changes in depth settings it is difficult to reset equally every time to keep the final depth uniform.

Illus. 27. Here the operator gradually widens the cut area by exerting downward pressure to keep the router base level on the uncut side and by taking light sideways cuts with back and forth strokes. The depth being cut here is over 3/4 inch.

Illus. 28 and 29. An example of a large, totally routed sign. This one is 5 feet wide by 7½ feet high. At right is a close-up of the "G" logo cut to two different depths. The entire logo was first cut to a ¼-inch depth. Then the border area was cut deeper (⅜ inch) with the router base supported only on the uncut area surrounding the logo.

Routing wide and deep can often be accomplished with even the lighter-weight routers. Patience is the key. Set your bit to the desired final depth. Start your cut safely away from the layout line. Hold the router tilted (tipped) on the edge of the router base so the bit is cutting comfortably shallower than the set depth. This technique is shown in Illustrations 25 and 26. Make several passes in this same general manner and in the same "cutting path" until the full depth is reached. Next, work the cut wider, bringing it precisely to the layout line. Continue stock removal until you get to the point where the router base is about to fall into the cutaway area. From here on you must exercise caution and concentrate diligently on what you are doing and what could happen should you become careless. Plan your stock removal sequence so that you will always have at least ½ to ⅓ of the router base supported on a flat uncut area. Maintain vertical pressure on that side of the router throughout the job to prevent the router from tipping or from "falling in." See Illustration 27. Routed letters of any large size can be handled this way. The same technique can be used to rout to more than one depth. See the example in Illustrations 28 and 29.

Sandblasting

The sandblasting process for making wood signs offers several major advantages over the other methods. In addition to the obvious features of unparalleled beauty and individuality, abrasive carving provides the opportunity for exquisite artistic expression. Fine, intricate details—in practically any size that can be outlined with a sharp knife—are easily reproduced with amazing accuracy. And, anyone can do it. See Illustrations 30–35.

The "short grain" areas of the wood are not as problematic in sandblasting as they are in hand carving and routing. Seldom, if ever, do you have to worry about the center areas popping out of small B's, O's, A's, and so on. Unlike other cutting methods, blasting can be done without regard to grain direction because the

Illus. 30 (above). Routed lettering and a sandblasted design make an interesting and pleasing combination of techniques in this still-to-be-painted sign. At first view, the design looks like an elegant carving.

Illus. 31 (left). A close-up of the sandblasted design. Notice the different "graining" resulting from each piece of wood. In this job the entire circle was routed to a smooth finish at a shallow depth before the stencil material was applied.

Illus. 32. Imagine the difficulty of routing or hand carving a job like this. Mike Maltby, a 15-year-old student, made this sign as his first school project. The pattern was copied from a fabric pennant.

wood is worn away by thousands of sand particles forced under high pressure to pulverize the individual wood fibres.

The major disadvantage of the blasting process is that special and, to date, somewhat unfamiliar equipment is involved. Most woodworking shops are not equipped with large enough air compressors and still fewer have sandblasters. However, after visiting many sign shops we have found that the lack of equipment does not deter many craftsmen from making sandblasted signs. They job the blasting work out to someone in their local area who specializes in sandblasting. If you are just starting to get into this, refer to *Making Wood Signs* and check with people listed in the yellow pages under sandblasting.

Illus. 33 (above). A plaque with raised letters, totally carved by sandblasting.

Illus. 34 (right). A sandblasted logo featuring relief design and incised lettering.

Illus. 35. A 4-foot-by-6-foot commercial sign cut entirely by sandblasting. Note the fine detail possible.

Since our previous book, *Making Wood Signs*, was published, one company has made available a new rubber stencil material developed especially for blasting wood signs. This new product is called Signblast Tape, and it is manufactured by Anchor Continental, Inc., 2000 S. Beltline Blvd., P.O. Drawer G, Columbia, S.C. 29250. Unlike the other stencils or mask previously used, this new material has a very aggressive adhesive tack. This feature makes it possible to use this tape on raw, unfinished wood without any auxiliary application of the contact cements (or fillers) that were previously necessary to assure good adhesion. These supplemental adhesives often left a sticky residue that was extremely difficult to remove from the raw wood.

One word of caution: The adhesive formula on the new stencil material may in fact be too aggressive for some soft woods and especially some prefinished panels. We have ruined several signs simply because we did not test first. For example, we were making some interior signs and had lacquered the surfaces before applying this new stencil material. After blasting we removed the stencil, taking along not only some of the lacquer surface finish, but also chips and slivers.

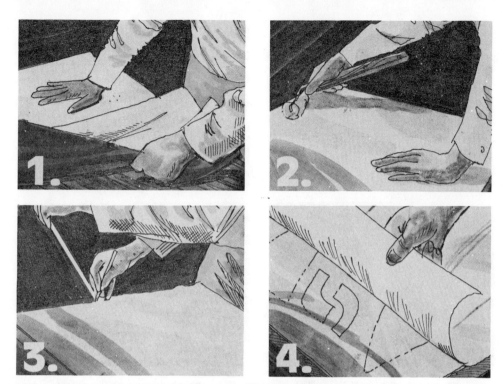

Illus. 36-39. Step 1 (top left). Place the Signblast Tape (cut slightly oversized) over the natural untreated wooden panel with the orange liner next to the wood. Strip the liner away as you pull, and apply the tape. Step 2 (top right). After the surface is completely covered with the Signblast Tape, burnish overall with a roller to remove wrinkles and to create an even bond. Step 3 (lower left). Trim excess stencil from the edges with a sharp knife or razor. Step 4 (lower right). Transfer your design, with carbon paper, to the surface of the stencil. (Continued on next page, see Illus. 40-43.)

The finish that did stay on the panels pulled the adhesive away from the back of the stencil, leaving us with a combination of problems and a real sticky mess.

On the other hand, we have had simply excellent results when applying this new stencil to raw redwood, cedars, pine, and so on. We have been somewhat successful using the new stencil on rough-sawn boards, too, but they must be touch-sanded first. The bond quality appears to be directly related to the degree of smoothness after sanding.

A step-by-step procedure of the sandblasting process using the new stencil material is outlined in Illustrations 36–43 (reprinted by permission of Anchor Continental, Inc.). This procedure is highly recommended for blasting raw wood (but with your own pretesting). For blasting prepainted, prevarnished, or pre-

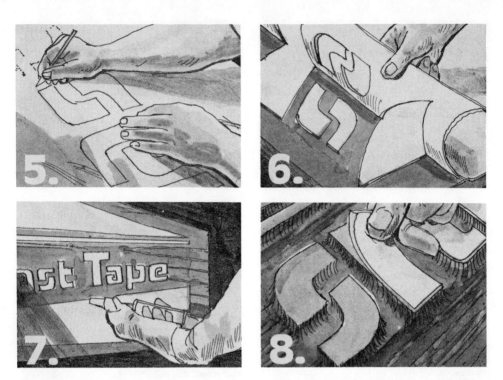

Illus. 40-43 (continued from previous page, Illus. 36-39). Step 5 (top left). Cut the stencil as usual from your transferred design. Step 6 (top right). Strip away the pattern, leaving the stencil applied only to the areas that are not to be blasted away. Step 7 (lower left). Blast to the depth desired to create a rich-looking carving. Step 8 (lower right). When blasting is completed, remove the stencil tape. If staining or spray painting of the blasted area is to be done, leave the tape on as a masking during this process, removing it later.

lacquered surfaces it is foolish not to test first. If the results appear questionable, we would recommend using the conventional stencils and supplemental adhesives as described in *Making Wood Signs*.

Hand Carving

There really isn't much new happening technically in the area of carved sign work. Artistically, however, it is another story. Many woodcarvers are comfortably edging their way into wooden sign work and setting new standards of skill, beauty, and overall excellence for all of us to behold. Our first ideas about carving wood signs were basically limited to two-dimensional letter work—that

Illus. 44. Sign artist Don Zinngrabe did all of this carved lettering using only two conventional, inexpensive carpenter's chisels (a medium and a narrow). This proves that skill is not in the tool, but in the hand of the artist.

is, either carving letters into a surface (Illus. 44 and 45) or removing backgrounds to raise the letters up in relief. The photos presented here will give you an overview of what is being done today and show you what is possible if you can carve. See Illustrations 46–50. You will notice that the lettering is still essentially "in" or "out" as usual, but the decorative designs and auxiliary flourishes

Illus. 45. Carved letter work by E. D. Hannaman.

Illus. 46 and 47. Two relief-carved signs by Dick Malacek, Weathertop Woodcraft. At left is a residential sign and at right is a family crest.

that complement the lettering add substantially to the uniqueness of hand-carved wood signage.

Other than a few new knives, chisel configurations, and small, lightweight power tools appearing on the market there really are not any new or magical tools or processes available to help you create three-dimensional effects. Our book *Making Wood Signs* gives the sign-carving basics and beyond that there are numerous other books on carving available to help you. (You can also refer to *Making Wood Signs* for information about carving machines.) Mastering wood-carving requires repetitious practice, continuous effort, and a burning desire to improve—all coupled with considerable patience. If you have or can develop the necessary personality traits (temperament), you have a lot of fun ahead. A vast array of different knives, chisels, and gouges is only secondary to the right mental approach. You can make a lot of fine carvings with just simple, basic tools—if you know how to use them as the experts do.

Pricing and the Sign Business

We have received endless phone calls and letters (far too many to answer) asking what to charge. This subject was intentionally omitted from our book *Making Wood Signs* simply because it is such a long, difficult, and ever-changing subject to deal with. Everyone has different expenses in tools, materials, types of

Illus. 48 (above). Another sign by Dick Malacek, Weathertop Woodcraft. This one, carved in butternut, was made for himself.

Illus. 49 (right). A 3-foot-by-7-foot carved sign with gold-leaf lettering, by Mary Sansoucy, The Signworks.

job orders, and so on. Individuals also have different levels of skill, expertise, and efficiency in their work. Furthermore, as we all know, wages and other costs constantly change and are anything but stable in this whirlwind economy.

Only you know (or can determine) what your actual costs are. Only you can determine what wage or salary you must have. Only you can determine what profit margin is necessary for reinvestment into your business.

If your real intent is to make a viable business out of this craft, we strongly suggest you seek some general business counselling: get the advice of your banker and visit an accountant or bookkeeper for help and assistance with your record keeping. You will need to calculate all of your overhead costs. This involves much more than just wood, glue, and paint. Your overhead includes such things as monthly rent or mortgage payments, taxes, insurance, and all utilities (including phone, electric, heat, and water). Tools, equipment, building depreciation, travel, hired help, and other supplies such as pencils, postage, stock material, and so on; all must be included on your list of expenses.

Convert all your yearly and monthly expenses to weekly, and then reduce them down to an hourly expense figure. This is your overhead and your fixed cost. On top of this add your own hourly wage plus the cost of the materials (include waste) involved in each job. On top of this add a percentage for profit. Profit can range from 20 to 100%. Profit is necessary as it provides the funding for the growth and expansion of your business. To do all of this requires lots of paper work and record keeping. Obviously, you must keep track of how long it takes to lay out, carve, rout, or blast signs. From all this data, you can then calculate a fair price based upon square or linear sign footage.

In general, we charge 35 to 40% more for engraved routed letter work than single-stroke routed letters. On double-faced signs, both routed and sandblasted, we charge 50 to 70% above the price of a single-faced sign, depending upon the material and detail involved.

As far as pricing is concerned, we strongly recommend *The Signwriter's Guide to Easier Pricing*, a reference book that deals with the average rates within the entire sign industry. This is an inexpensive little shirt-pocket-size booklet that is updated frequently. It gives current hourly rates for all aspects of sign work. For example, it specifies the suggested hourly trade rates for all phases of art work, painting, and sign installation, along with specific pricing data for routed and sandblasted signs of all sizes. A section is also devoted to charges for cutout

Illus. 50. Intricate carving detail by Paul McCarthy's Carving Place, Scituate, Massachusetts.

letters in different heights and materials. This valuable little booklet has been the Blue Book of the sign industry for almost a decade. It can be ordered from the Signwriter's Publishing Co., 807 Ave. C, Billings, MT 59102.

If you do a lot of the repetitive small residential name signs you can make up an illustrated price list and order form. A simplified version similar to one we still use is shown in Illustration 51. Simply lay out the sample shapes and list any options and special charges that are relative to your own operation. Once done, have the original reproduced by photocopy or instant printing. With carbon paper you can give your customer a copy and keep one copy for your work orders and income records. Above all, it is very important to keep track of all of your costs, both for establishing your own pricing and for your tax deductions.

You will not make it by accepting less than a fair price just to get a job or to undercut a competitor. We don't worry about the wood sign maker just down the road who charges less. He will soon tire of working for nothing (as would you) and eventually close his operation. Keep your prices up there—at least comparable to those of the skilled tradespeople in your area. If you are conscientious and put out quality signs you will not have to worry. You will get repeat business from satisfied customers. Having signs representative of your best efforts out there in the public's eye is your best advertising.

Doing the larger signs presents more risks, especially if you do not price them right. Clients who intend to order a large sign want to know their cost before you start. Avoid giving quick verbal prices unless you are "dead sure." We have found that it is just good business to give prices for larger signs in writing (that is, as a written quotation).

Pricing begins with a consultation with the prospective customer to establish what he actually wants. Then, when you're alone, take the time to slowly think through the job. Do your calculations and double check—you do not want to miss anything. Put your quotation in the form of a letter and mail it to the prospect.

Some specifications to include in your quotation are the overall size, one or two sides, kind of materials, how assembled, style and size of letters, if and how finished and if delivery, installation (any electrical), and whether or not local taxes are included. It is also a good idea to develop a standard statement of disclaimer with regard to certain liabilities, such as zoning ordinances, installation, service life, and so on. This makes it clear to the customer that he assumes all such relevant liabilities. Another important subject to spell out very clearly in your quotation letter is the financial terms. It is not unreasonable to ask for an advance of 50% with the order and the balance to be paid on completion. Avoid extending credit. Finally, it is only fair to the customer to state the time you will need to complete the job, such as "3 to 4 weeks to completion."

Subcontracting. Remember that your ultimate objective is to put out only good signs and to do them as financially equitably as possible for yourself and your client. Rather than risk your reputation by doing a job, or part of a job, that just

NAME:_____

ADDRESS: _____

_____

PHONE: _____ PICK-UP:_____

SMALL SIGNS: (W/BLACK SPRAY PAINT)
(SMOOTH SURFACE)

A. SMALL
(1" x 4" x 16")

B. MEDIUM
(1" x 6" x 18")

C. LARGE
(1" x 8" x 20")

ADD # FOR SHAPES B & C

SHAPE	SIZE	1-SIDE	2-SIDES
	SMALL	#	#
	MEDIUM	#	#
	LARGE	#	#

ADDITIONAL CHARGE FOR MORE THAN ONE LINE.
ADDITIONAL CHARGE FOR LARGER SIGNS.
ALL PRICES PLUS % TAX

Illus. 51. A simplified version of a combination order form and price list for standardized name signs.

doesn't measure up, explore the possibility of subcontracting. That is, simply hire someone to do the work for you that you are not equipped to handle yourself. If you have problems with layout, hire an artist, designer, or sign painter. If you are not equipped to prepare and glue-up large panels, go to a cabinet shop. There certainly isn't anything wrong with going to another sign shop to hire airbrush or gold-leaf work. Be sure to get a firm price beforehand so you can include it in the quotation to your client. Add 10 to 20% extra for your legwork, time, and paper work. It is almost impossible to be all-skilled and all-efficient in all areas of a wood sign business. One day you will get a request for a routed sign with raised gold-leaf letters, the next day it is a sandblasted job with airbrush, and so it goes.

Trade Publications. In order to keep abreast of what is going on in the sign trade around the country, you will want authoritative, current information. There are two excellent publications well worth examining. One is *Signs of the Times*, a monthly magazine available from Signs of the Times Publishing Co., 407 Gilbert Ave., Cincinnati, OH 45202. The other is a fairly new quarterly publication called *Sign Craft*, available from Sign Craft, P.O. Box 06031, Fort Myers, FL 33906. Both magazines allot plenty of space to wood signs, contain relevant how-to articles, and are valuable sources for locating special supplies. They also sponsor sign design awards, give association notices, and often publish a cost or pricing analysis for wood signs.

Alphabets and
Design Patterns

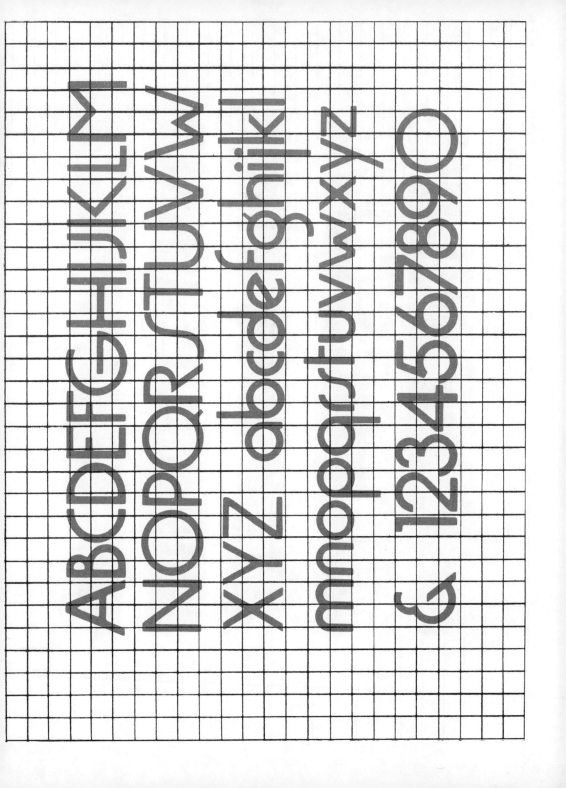
ABCDEFGHIJKLM
NOPQRSTUVW
XYZ abcdefghijkl
mnopqrstuvwxyz
& 1234567890

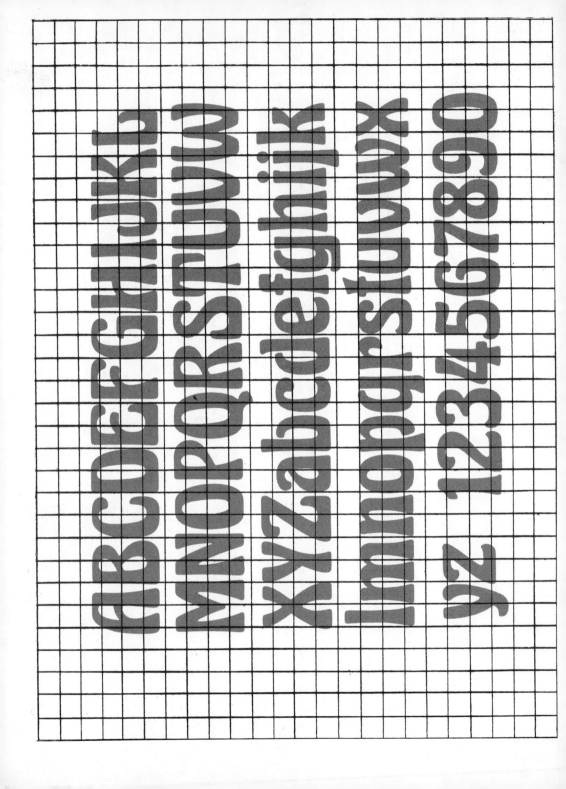

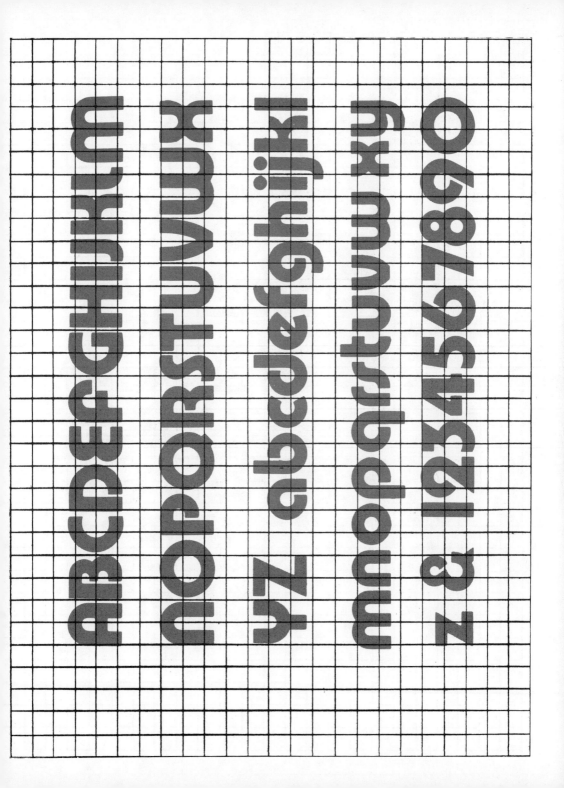

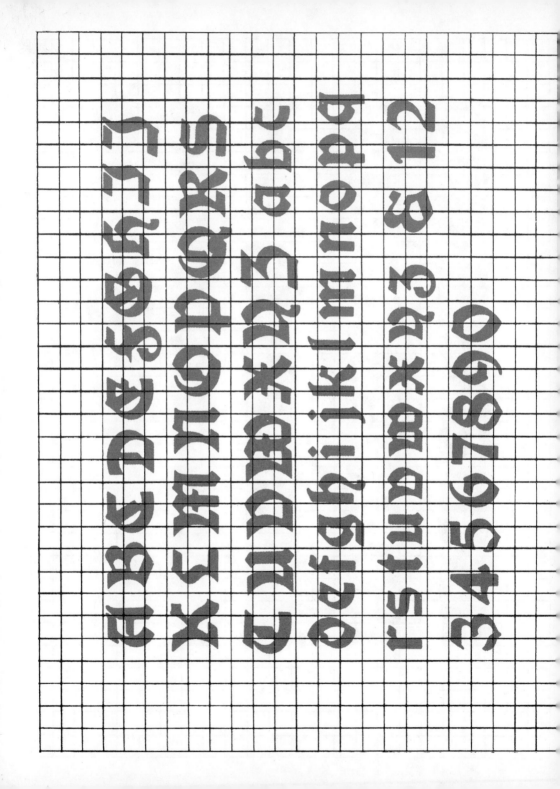

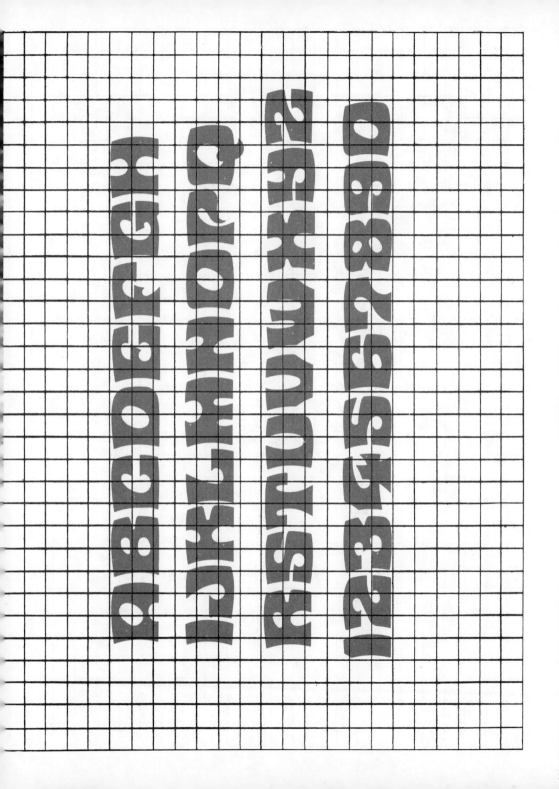

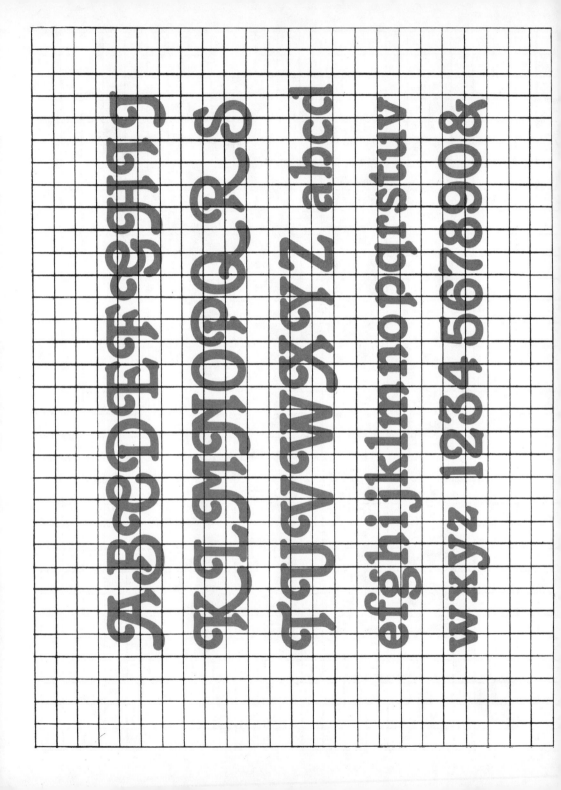

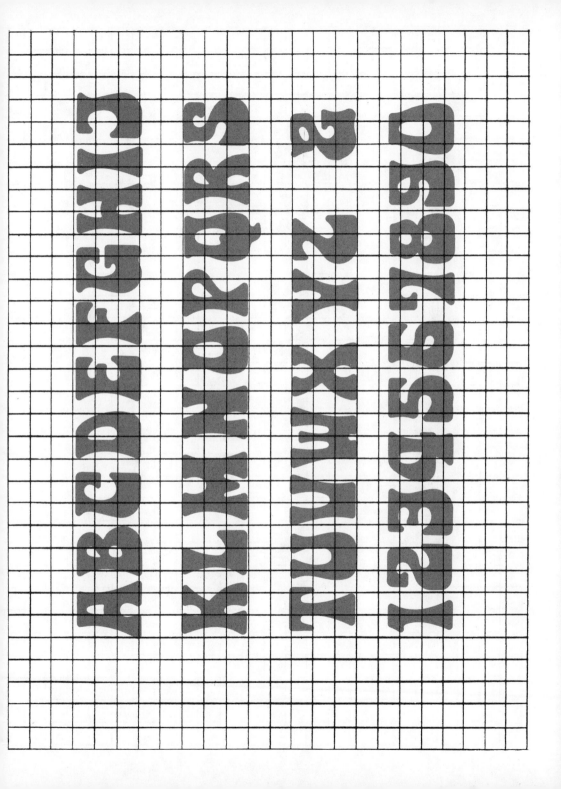

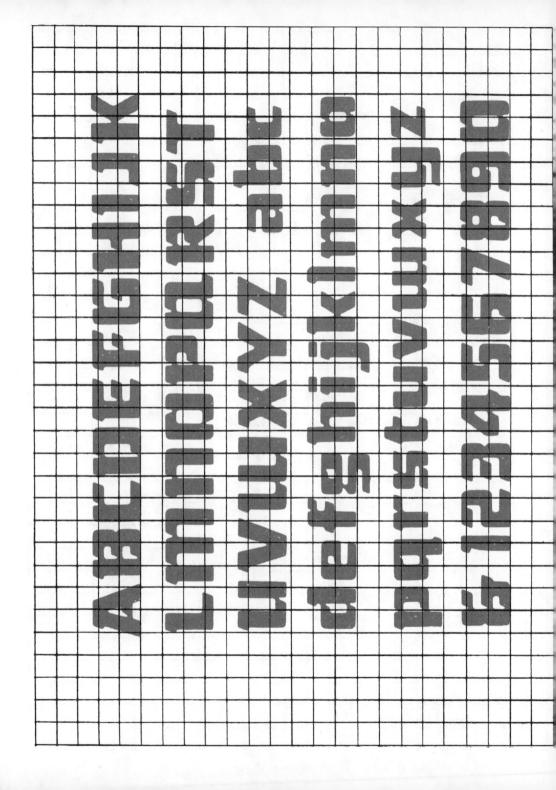

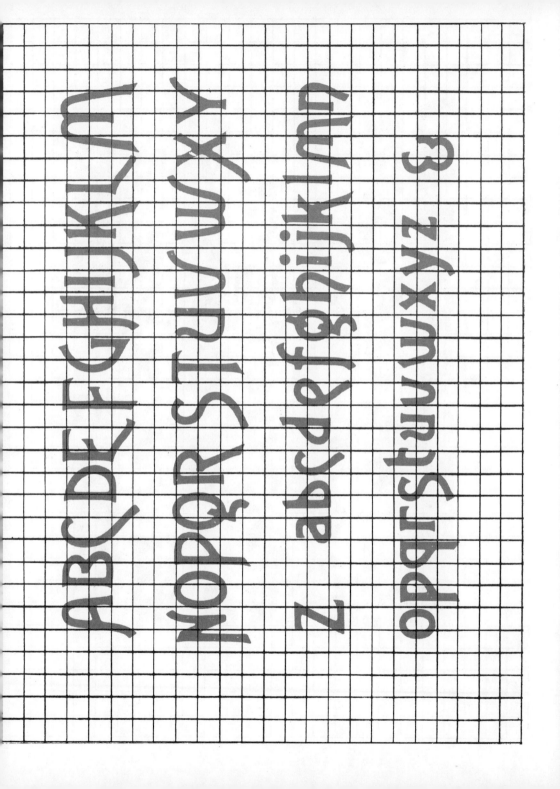

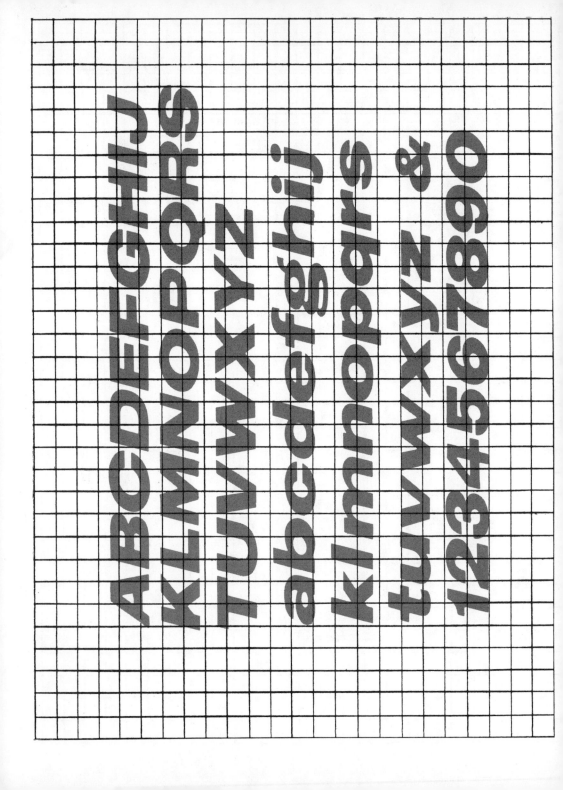

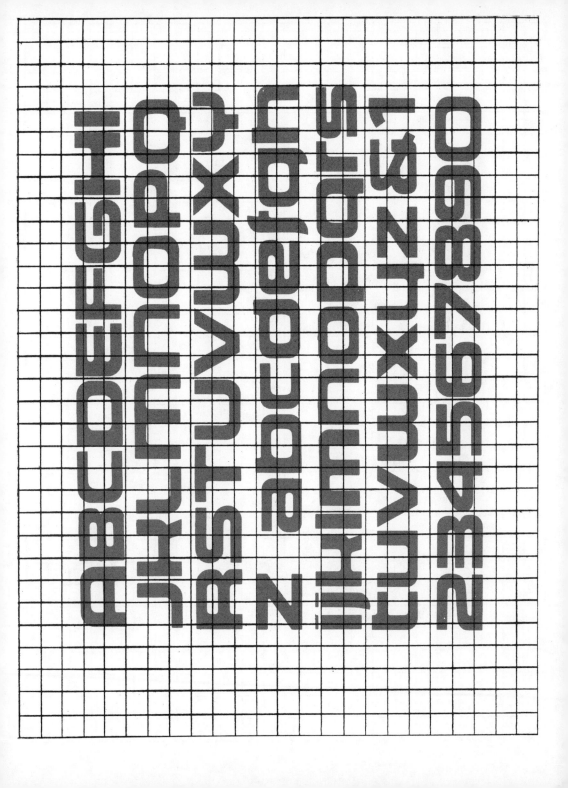

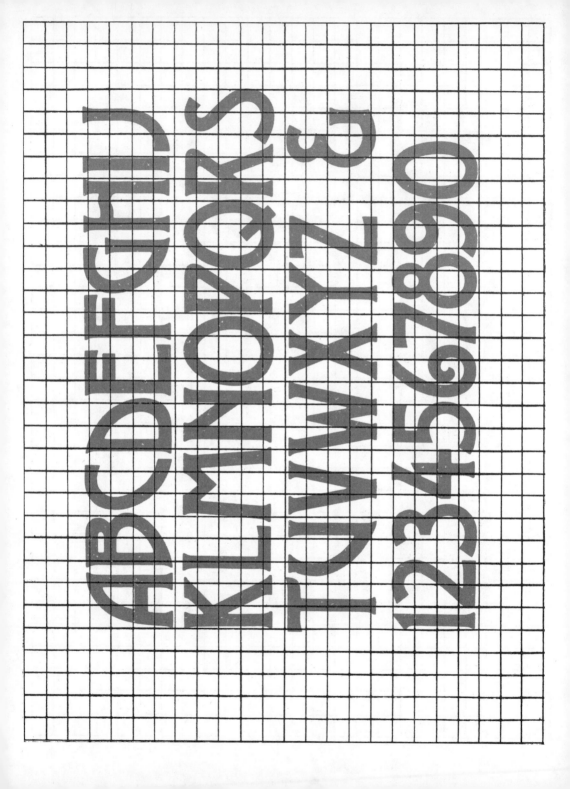

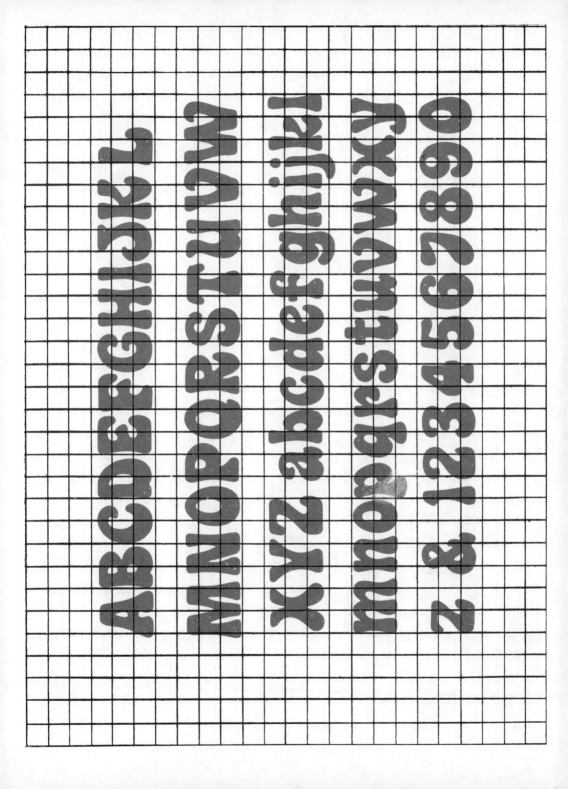

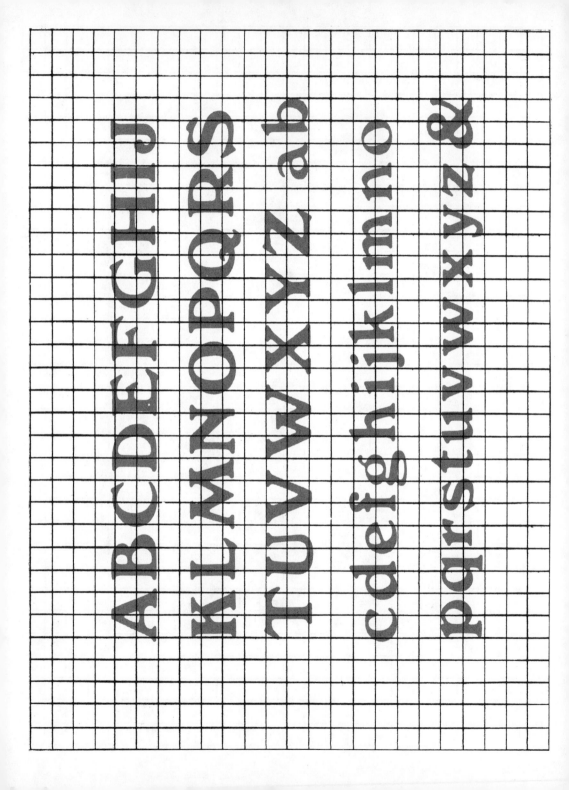

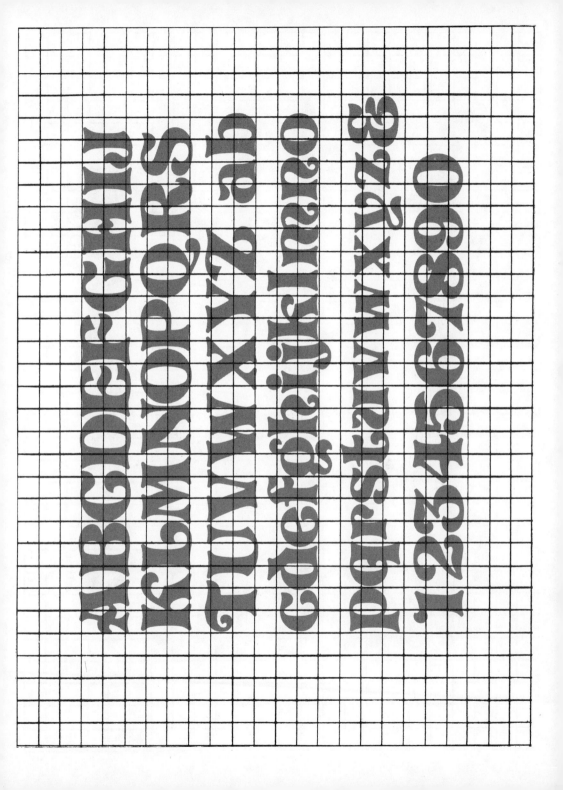

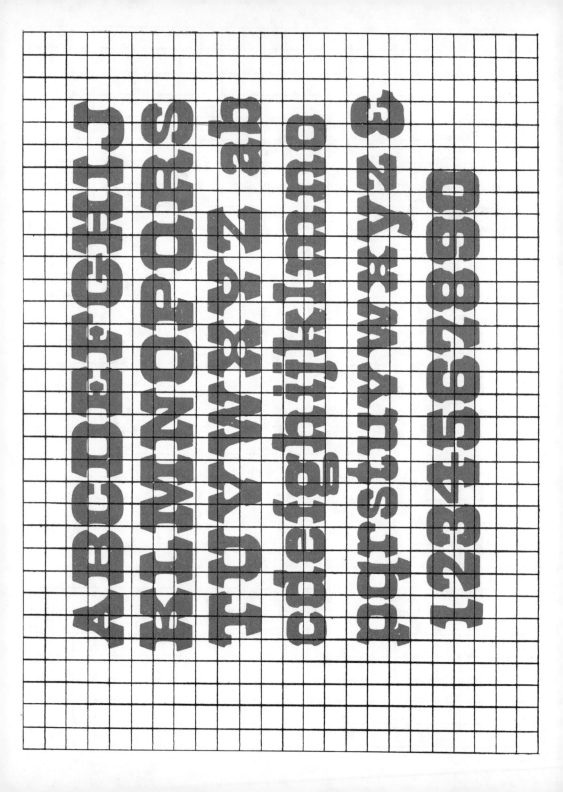

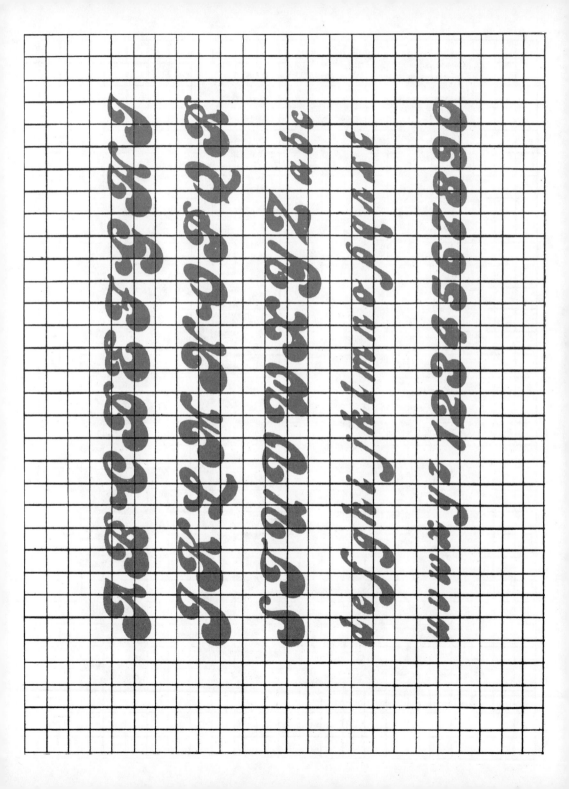

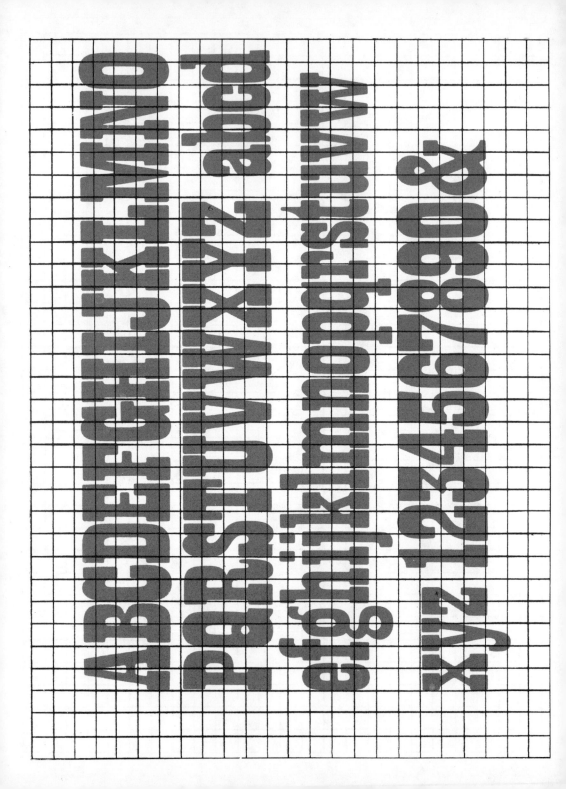

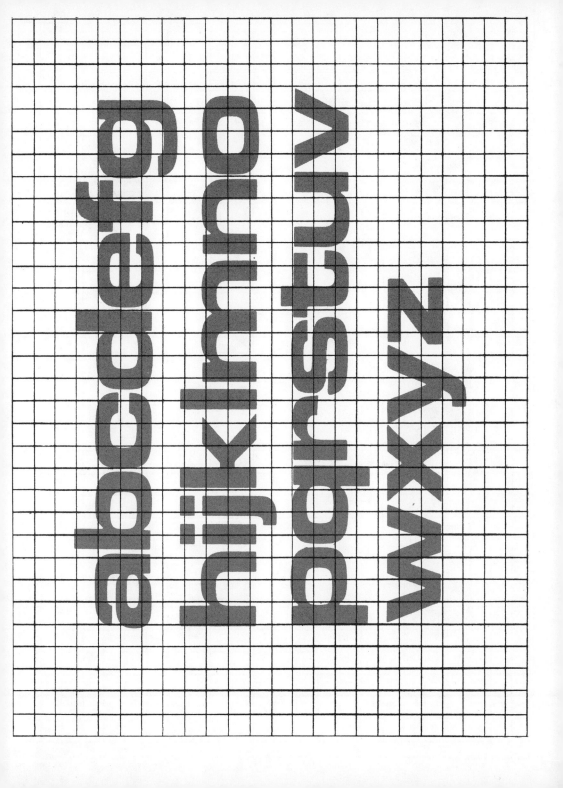

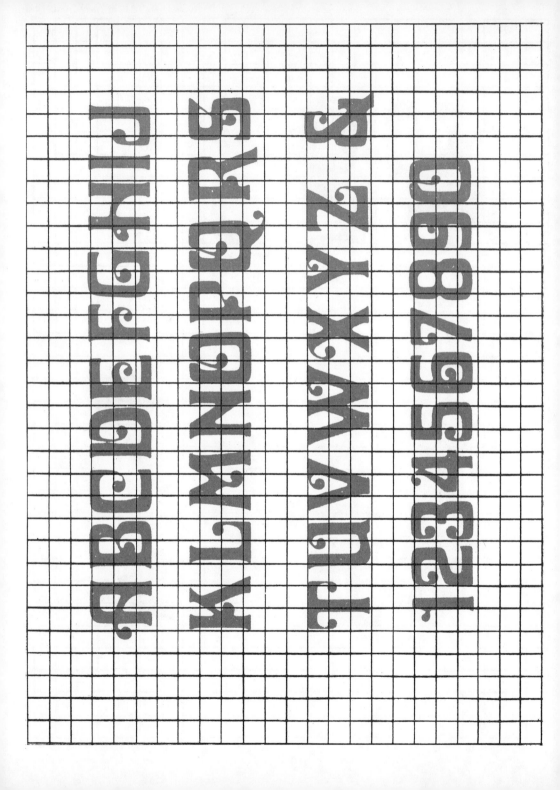

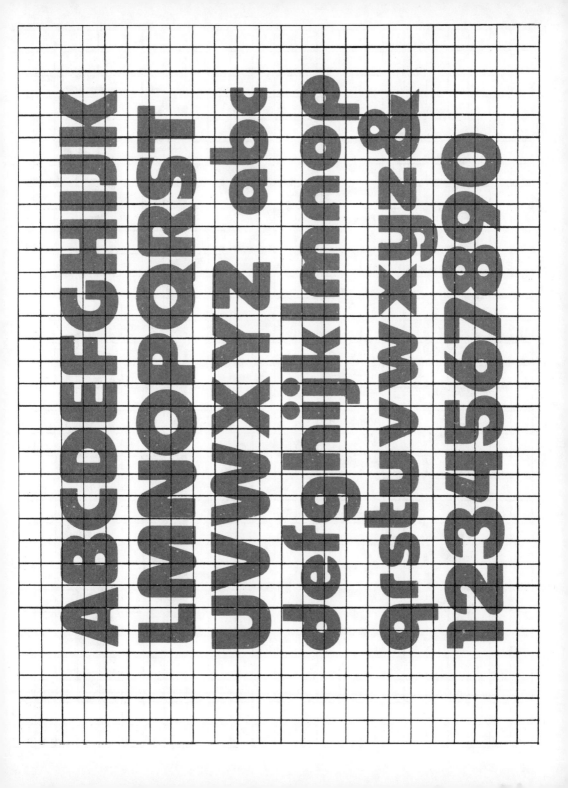

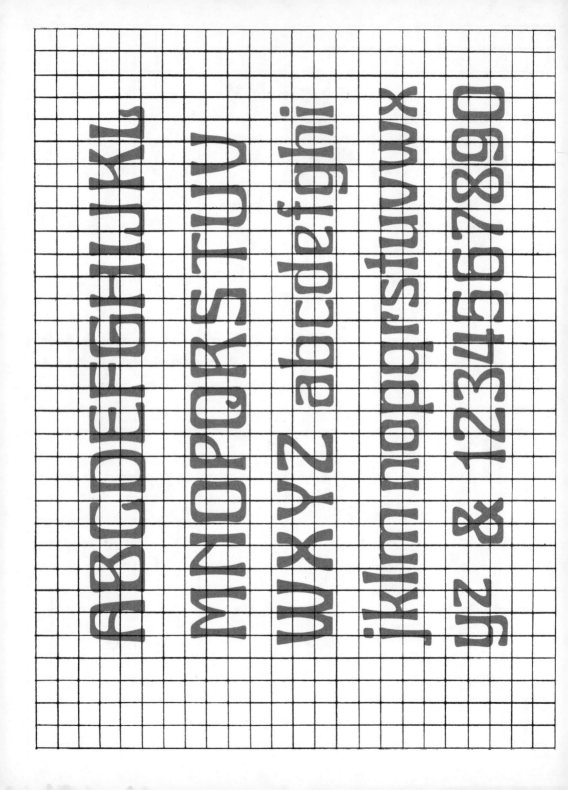

ABCDEFGHIJKL
MNOPQRSTUV
WXYZ abcdefghi
jklmnopqrstuvwx
yz & 1234567890

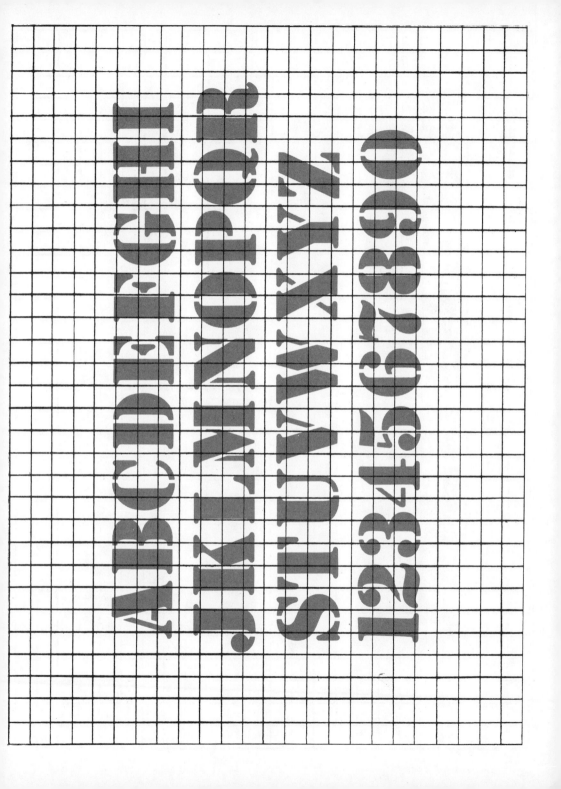

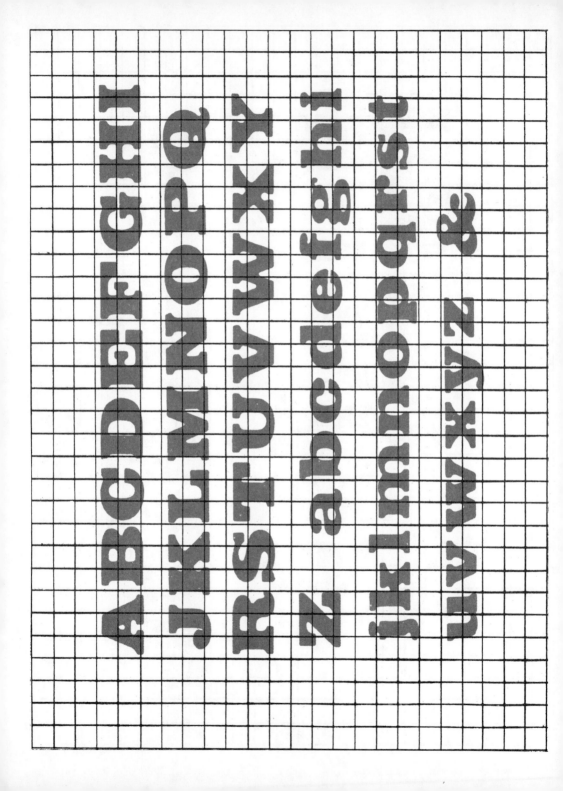

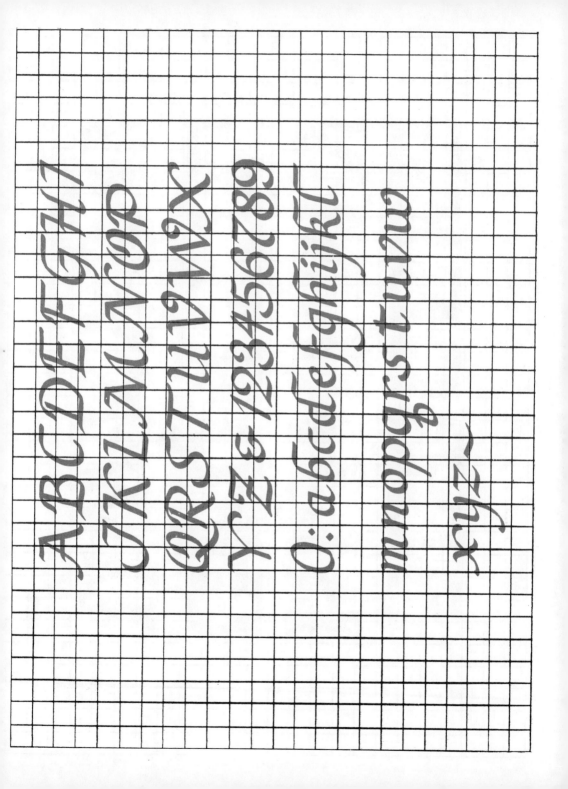

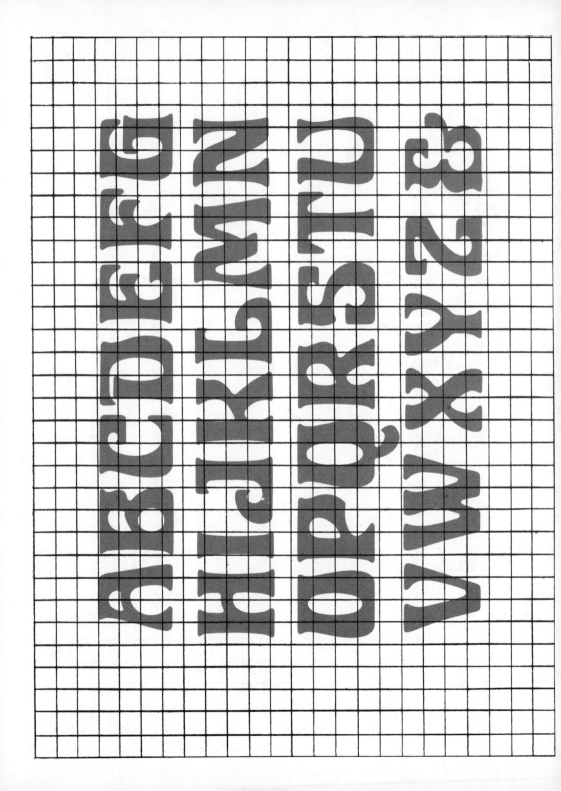

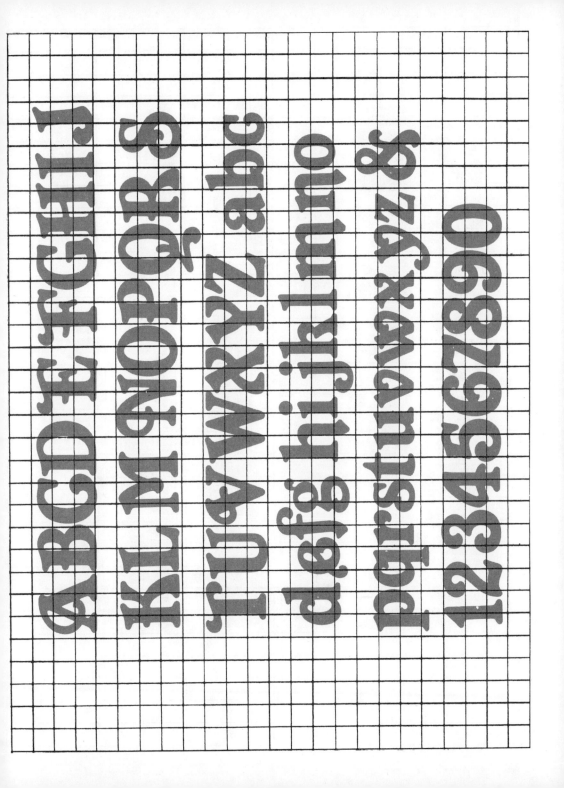

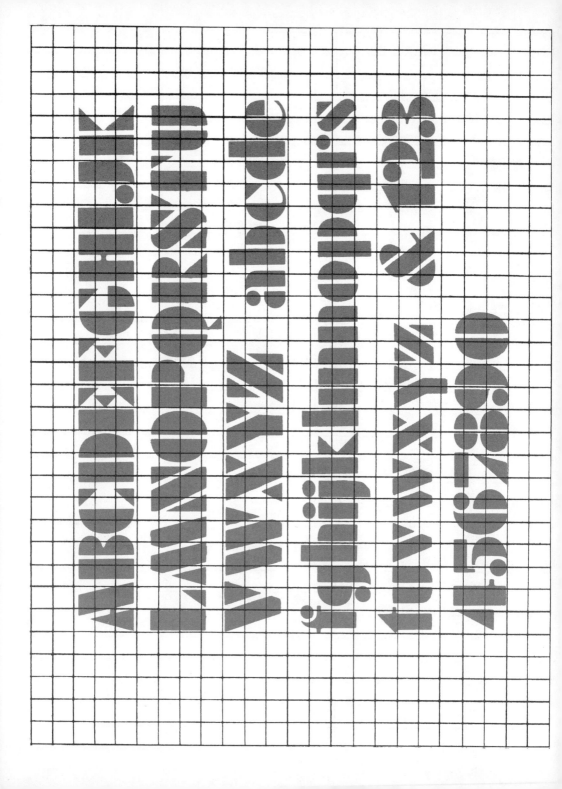

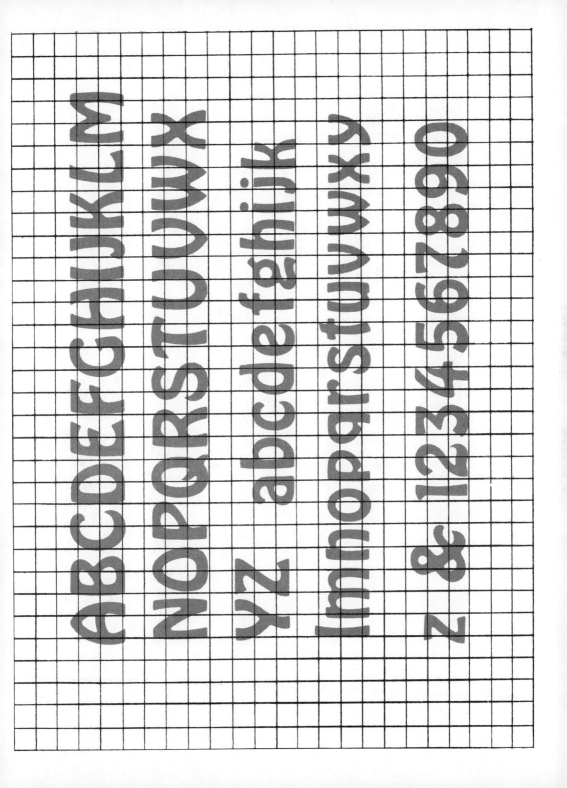

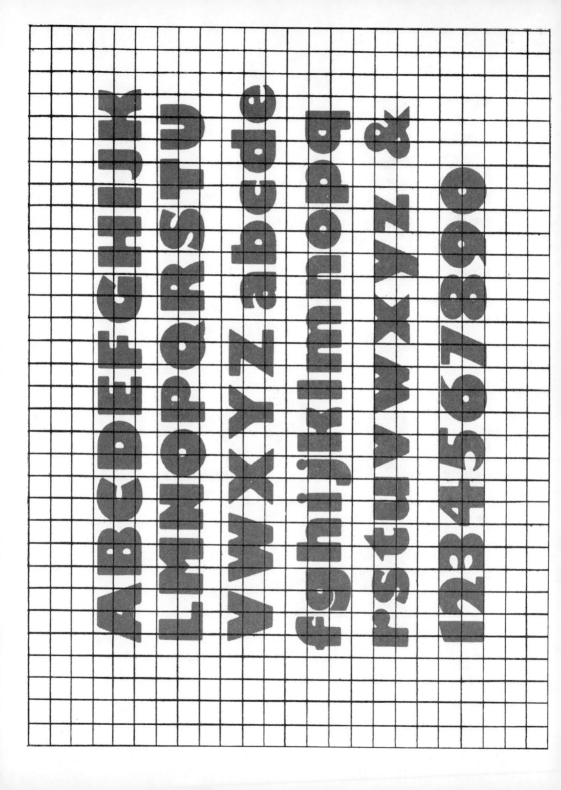

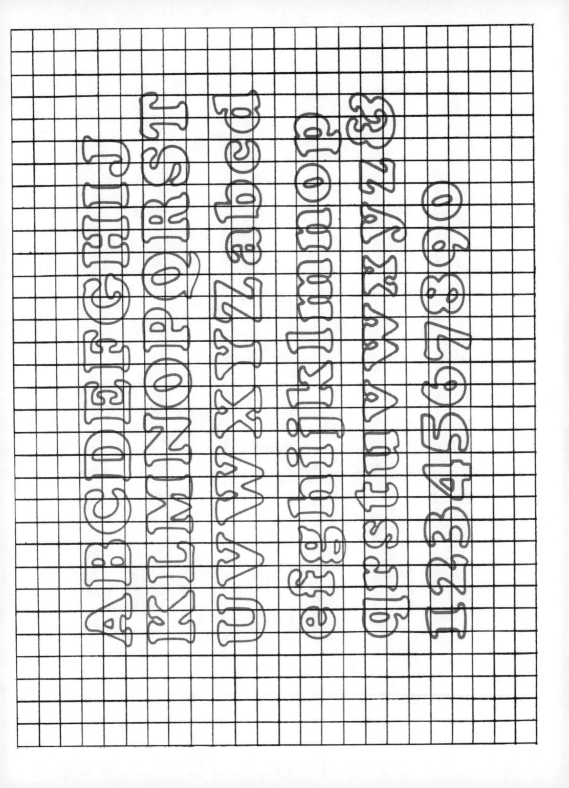

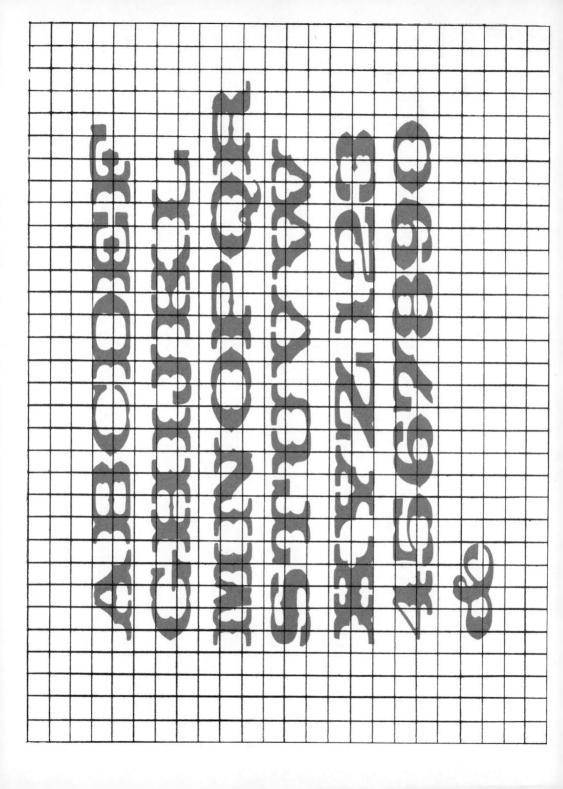

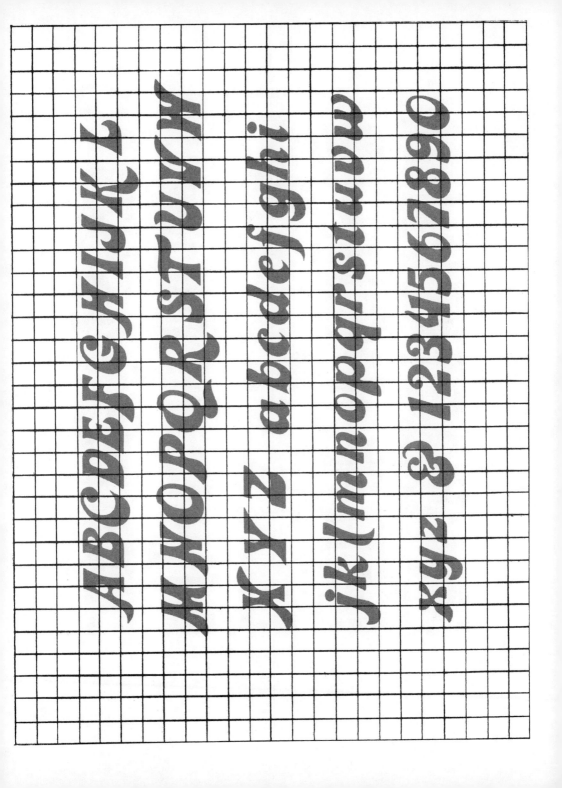

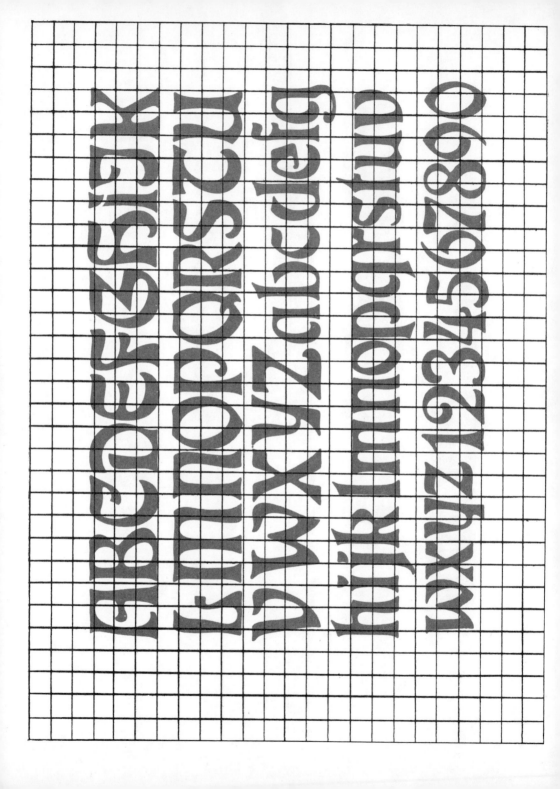

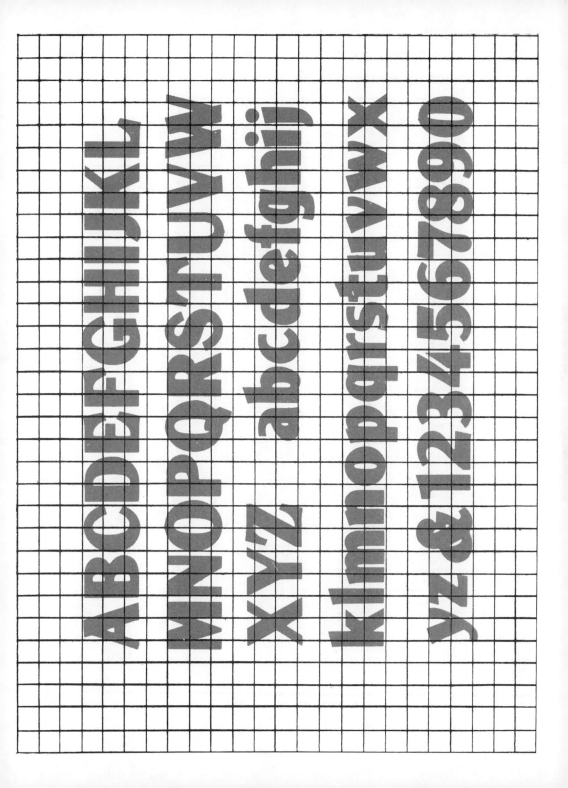

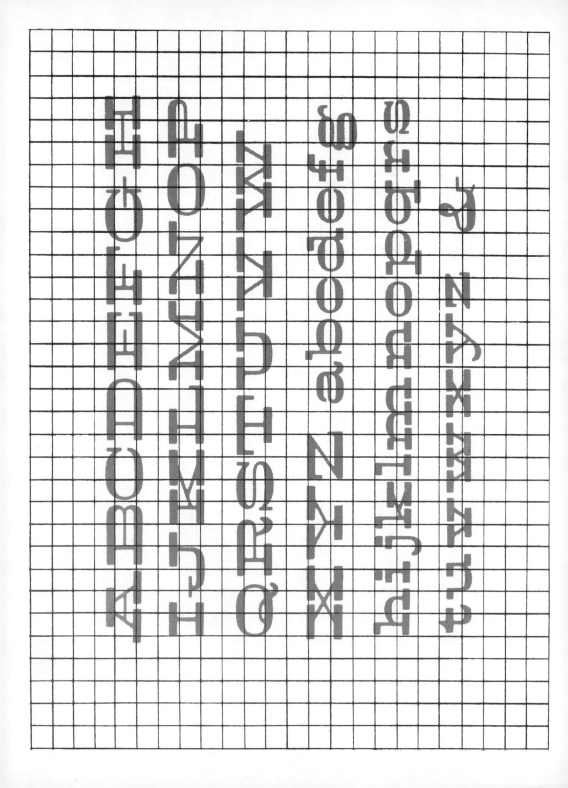

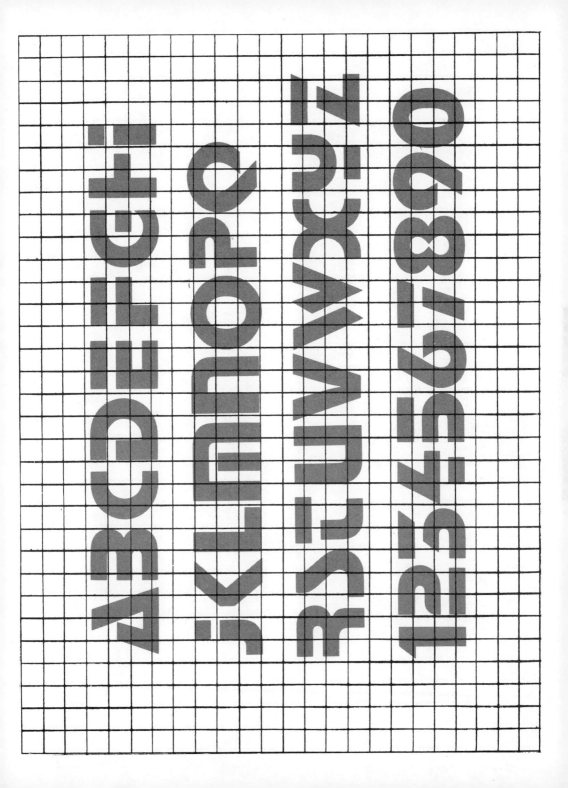

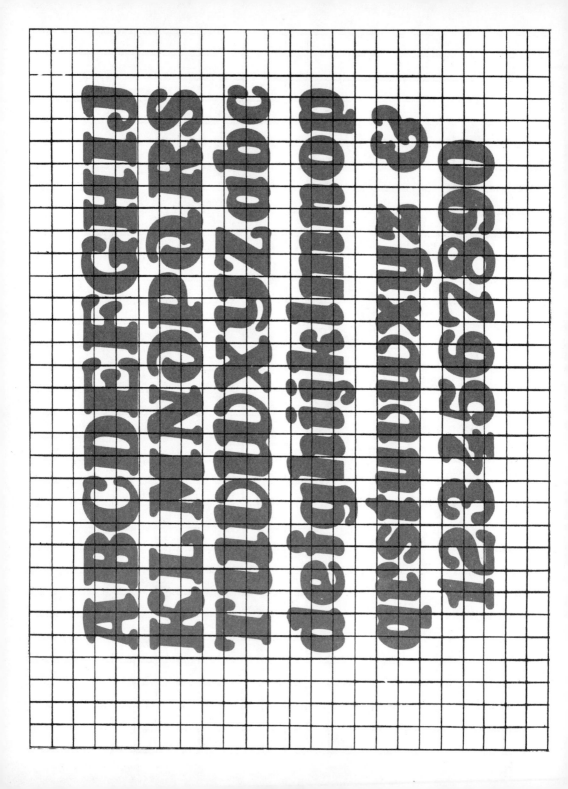

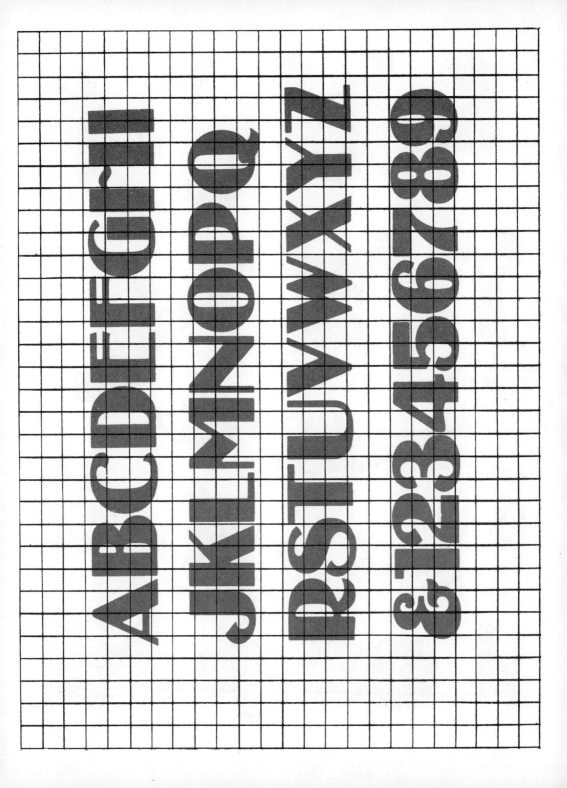

Photo Gallery
of Wood Signs

Routed and hand-carved redwood, gloss enamel painted, by Spielmans Wood Works.

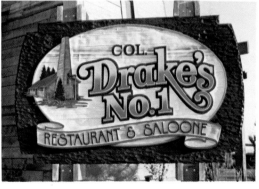

Three signs by Mike Jackson, Jackson Signs, Inc. Sign at upper right combines cutout applied wood letters and art with carved textured background. The others combine carving and sandblasting.

A

Three signs by Spielmans Wood Works. Sign at top is sandblasted redwood, painted and stained. At left is routed rough-sawn cedar, natural and painted. Sign below is routed cedar, stained and painted.

B

Sandblasted redwood, natural and painted, by Spielmans Wood Works.

Sandblasted sign by Don Davis, Wildwood Signs, Div., Lowen Co.

Hand-carved oak, stained, by William J. Schnute, Oak Leaves Studio.

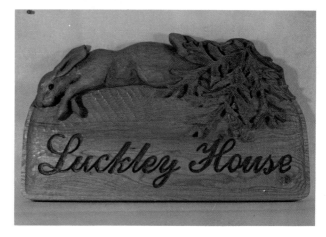

Five signs, combining various elements of carving, sandblasting, painting, and staining, by Wayne Detjen, Wood Graphics Div., Wis. Label Corp.

D

(Above) Sign and post work by Mike Jackson, Jackson Signs, Inc.

(Right) Sandblasted sign in Michigan. Note the rope border. (Designer and fabricator unknown.)

(Left) Sign by Wayne Detjen, Wood Graphics Div., Wis. Label Corp.

(Below) A sign displaying the multiple woodworking talents of Mike Jackson.

A closeup look at a painting detail from a Mike Jackson sign that also features sandblasting and hand-carved detailing.

Sandblasted 2-inch pine, 8 feet by 7½ feet, by Brian Bagliss, The Sign Center.

Tongue-and-groove pine backing, 3 feet by 16 feet with cutout and painted plywood letters. By Brian Bagliss, The Sign Center.

Sandblasted sign by Mike Jackson, Jackson Signs, Inc.

Another of Mike Jackson's signs.

Sandblasted sign by Wayne Detjen, Wood Graphics Div., Wis. Label Corp.

CHIROPRACTIC OFFICE

Dr. D.G. Kenny

Dr. B. A. Otto

1421 LAKE ST.

Standing sign, carved by Mary Sansoucy, The Signworks.

Sandblasted sign by Wayne Detjen, Wood Graphics Div., Wis. Label Corp.

Two sandblasted signs by Mike Jackson, Jackson Signs, Inc.

Sign by Mike Jackson, Jackson Signs, Inc.

Carved and sandblasted sign by Dick Malacek, Weathertop Woodcraft.

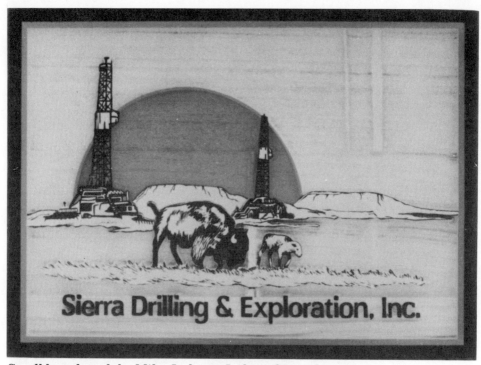

Sandblasted work by Mike Jackson, Jackson Signs, Inc.

Sandblasted sign by Ron Reedy, Reedy's Sign & Design.

Sandblasted sign by Wayne Detjen, Wood Graphics Div., Wis. Label Corp.

Sandblasted sign by Mike Jackson.

Sandblasting and router work by Wayne Detjen.

Another excellent design by Mike Jackson.

Freehand single-stroke routing in rough cedar.

Hand-carved sign, 3½ feet by 7 feet, by Mary Sansoucy, The Signworks.

Sandblasted sign in Florida. (Designer and fabricator unknown.)

Sign exemplifying the woodworking and graphic talents of Mike Jackson, Jackson Signs, Inc.

Sandblasted sign by Wayne Detjen, Wood Graphics Div., Wis. Label Corp.

Golf course signage by Carl Rauwerdink, Old Oak Shop, Inc.

Routed sign by Wayne Detjen.

Sandblasted sign by Mike Jackson, Jackson Signs, Inc.

(Below) Routing in unfinished cedar.

Routed and hand carved, 30-inch diameter, by Carl Rauwerdink, Old Oak Shop, Inc.

Routed and sandblasted work by Mike Jackson.

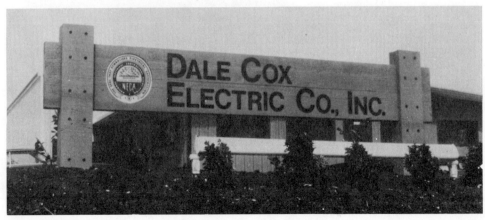

(Left) By Buzz Bizzell, Sunshine Wooden Sign Co., Charlotte, North Carolina.

(Below) A clean, contemporary sign, routed and with a sandblasted logo, by Mike Jackson, Jackson Signs, Inc.

Sign by The Heron Co., Foxboro, Massachusetts.

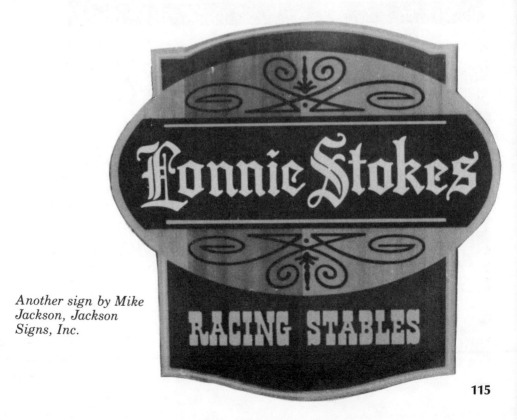

Another sign by Mike Jackson, Jackson Signs, Inc.

(Above) Sign by Mike Jackson,
Jackson Signs, Inc.

(Left) Cutout letter work by Wayne
Detjen, Wood Graphics Div., Wis.
Label Corp.

Sandblasted sign by Ron Reedy, Reedy's Sign & Design.

Closeup detail of Ron Reedy's eagle. Made of 2-inch redwood backed with ⅝-inch exterior plywood, it was profile sawn, with lines blasted in, and air brushed with Japan colors to create a soft effect.

This sign by Mike Jackson involved woodturning, woodcarving and sandblasting.

Carved sign by Oceanic Arts, Whittier, California.

(Below) Sign by Mike Jackson, Jackson Signs, Inc.

Wall-mounted sign by Mike Jackson.

(Left) An interesting sign by Mike Jackson.

Sign by Wayne Detjen, Wood Graphics Div., Wis. Label Corp.

(Above) Sandblasted ground sign by Ron Reedy, Reedy's Sign & Design.

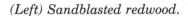

(Left) Sandblasted redwood.

(Below) Designed by Gerard Ryan of Cherry Lane Studios, Toronto, Ontario, this sign is 2½ feet by 20 feet, 5 inches thick, made of laminated cedar, with sandblasted lettering and logo.

Blasting and carving highlight this sign by Mike Jackson.

Sandblasted sign by Lew Morrison Signs, Hayes, Virginia.

Sign by Kum Giordano, Creator's Touch, Wrentham, Massachusetts.

Sandblasted sign by Parkway Products, McHenry, Illinois.

Sandblasted pine with changeable hours board, by Eagle Sign & Adv. Co., Des Moines, Iowa.

Sign by Mike Jackson, Jackson Signs, Inc., Moore, Oklahoma. Note the real rope used for a border.

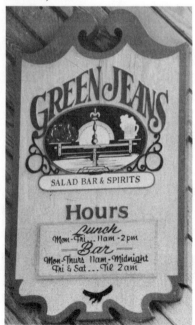

(Above) Sandblasted redwood corporate sign, 33 inches by 8 feet overall, by Ron Reedy, Reedy's Sign & Design.

(Left) This sign by Robert M. Lavche, Taos, New Mexico, combines applied raised letters and decorative carving.

(Above) Sandblasted redwood, 2 inches thick, 3 feet by 6 feet. Designed by Dan Ward and Terry Hubs of Chaparral Signs, San Martin, California.

(Right) Artistic work by Steven Garrity, Garrity Carved Signs, Belmont, Massachusetts.

Massive sign by Modesto Commercial Graphics, Ceres, California.

Hand-carved pine, designed by Martha Williams, The Wood Shop, Boyne City, Michigan.

Sign by E. D. Hannaman, E. D. Hannaman Sign Crafters, Newville, Pennsylvania.

A huge sign, 4 feet by 34 feet, carved in oak with rounded face wood letters applied. Design by Ann Thurston, The Wood Shop, Boyne City, Michigan.

Cher Flores of the Rustic Sign Studio, Denver, Colorado, combined carving, sandblasting and woodturning to make this sign.

Carved signage by La Barge Gallery, Conway, New Hampshire.

Index